Stephanie Liggins

1

I Hear Their Cries

I HEAR THEIR CRIES

STEPHANIE LIGGINS

Copyright

Library of Congress
Cataloging-in-Publication Data
ISBN: 979-8-9885825-1-9

Cole Publishing
4067 Hardwick Street #282
Lakewood, CA 90712
Email: ccpprod@aol.com

Book Cover Design by Covenant Images
For Book Orders:
Contact us at Cole Publishing Company

Cole Publishing

Dedication

I dedicate this book to all the children whose voices have been silenced by the pain of separation from their birth parents. Lift your heads high, because you have a heavenly Father who is willing to adopt you. Psalms 27:10

Special Thanks

Reflecting on my incredible journey, I am humbled and inspired by my progress and just how far I have come. My humble beginnings truly set an example that you can be anything you want to be in this world.

I want to thank my sister and publisher Dr. Candace Cole-Kelly for her unwavering love, boundless wisdom, and divine inspiration that has been my constant companion in this creative endeavor. Your guidance has been a beacon of light through the highs and lows, illuminating my path and filling me with the strength to persevere. I am in awe of the blessings with just how much my Heavenly Father has showered His grace upon me. I wholeheartedly acknowledge that this book would not have been possible without His Divine intervention.

Moreover, I am immensely grateful for my son "Alex," who encouraged me and kept me centered with my eyes focused on my life goals. To my Granddaughter Elizabeth, your affection has shaped my writing and given me the strength to see this project through. I wish to extend my gratitude to all those who have supported and encouraged me throughout this journey. Your unwavering belief in me has been an invaluable source of strength. Thank you to my family, friends, and mentors.

Lastly, may this book serve to reach every reader and uplift their hearts and spirits through the boundless love poured into this project.

Thank you, dear Heavenly Father, for your presence in my life and for making this dream a reality. With a heart filled with reverence and thanksgiving, I offer this book as a tribute to Your Infinite Grace and Guidance.

Stephanie Liggins

Introduction

Did you know that foster care is a *temporary living situation* for children whose parents cannot take care of them and whose need for care has come to the attention of the Child Welfare Agency staff? You may also not know that while in foster care, children may live with relatives, foster families or in group home/facilities.

In the stories you will read about, the names of some individuals have been omitted and some identifying characters have been changed and a few select portrayals are composites.

Foster Care Population at end of year

I would like to share some very important information with you regarding children that are in the "system" as provided by the Department of Health and Human Services: The number of children currently in foster care is counted every year on September 30th, the end of the fiscal year. Children, however, enter and exit the foster care system all year long and this means that the figures frequently change. The total foster care population at the end of the 2021 year was 391,098, (which represented a decrease of 16,220, or 3.98%, from 2020.)

Stephanie Liggins

I have listed a few items for your further review regarding the foster care system as follows:

1) Age Group
2) Race and Ethnicity

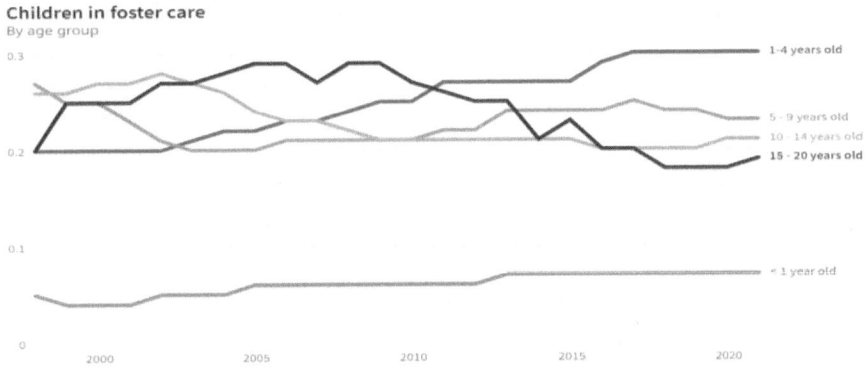

Sources: Department of Health and human services.

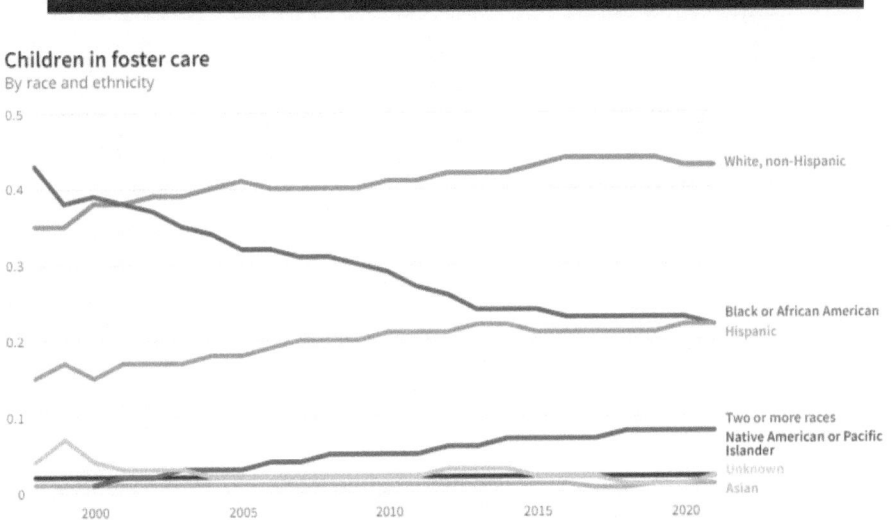

Data from both the regular and revised AFCARS file submissions received by August 10, 2018, are included in the following listings. Missing data is excluded from each table. Therefore, the totals within each distribution may not equal the total provided for that subpopulation (e.g. number in care on September 30th may not match the sum across ages for that group).

Chapter 1

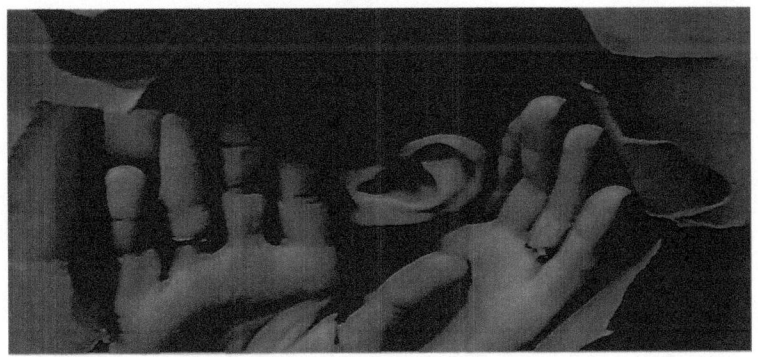

Tears of Longing

It was a sunny Thursday afternoon when I transported this beautiful six-year-old girl. Let's call her Sally; she had beautiful, brown-toned skin, shoulder length curly hair, big brown eyes and a beautiful smile topping it all off. She had been eager that morning-to go see her family.

When I picked her up for the visit, she softly asked, "Are you going to take me to see my mom?" I smiled and said, "Yes I am," as she ran to put her shoes on.

She wore blue shorts, a colorful t-shirt and had a Band-Aid on one knee. After putting her shoes on, she ran back towards me and reached for my hand ready to leave for our adventure. We held hands as we walked to the car swinging them back and forth in unison. I placed her small-framed body in the car seat, securing her with the seat belt and took my seat. She asked if I was going to pick up her "Bro, Bro" [her biological brother]. I told her that he was our next stop and boy, was she excited!

Sally couldn't wait to see him and continued every few minutes to ask if we were there yet. I finally got her to sit back, enjoy the music from the radio, the passing surroundings and convinced her that I would let her know when we got close. She was such a sweet child.

After what seemed an eternity, we finally got to the Group Home, and she excitedly asked, "Does my Bro, Bro live here?" I finally was able to say, "yes he does." As I exited the car, she wanted to know if she could run ahead to the door, but I told her to wait in the car until I got further instructions. She smiled really big as she poked her head out the window of the car. She loved her "Bro, Bro."

I walked towards the house occasionally glancing back to watch the anticipation in her eyes. Sally was wishing hard that her Bro, Bro would magically appear. Then suddenly, he ran out! When she saw him, she started to scream his name, Bro, Bro! Her face appeared to be glowing as he entered the car, and she was full of all kinds of questions! She told him, "We are going to see mom." She talked a mile a minute as she excitedly told him how much she missed him!

When we arrived at their mom's location, Bro Bro jumped out of the car while I helped Sally to get out. As soon as I turned, their momma was right there, loving, hugging and crying with joy to see them. The children began sharing conversation with their mom! The mother was just as happy as the kids as they laughed and giggled, touching one another!

The hours rolled by, and finally, it was time to leave. Immediately the little girl's emotional and facial expressions changed as she could feel the time winding down. Mom tried to keep her attitude up, but Sally was hardly ready to say goodbye!

Mom comforted Bro Bro first as he began to cry, she held him close to her breast as tears rolled down her face. The kids knew they had to leave but they moved very slowly dragging out the time trying to make it last as long as possible.

It broke my heart over and over again watching all three of them cling to each other as long as possible. It was both Bro, Bro and Mom who had to help Sally get into the car. They kissed and hugged each other through the window and their momma promised she would see the children again real soon.

Reluctantly, Sally took her seat in the car with tears still rolling down her face. Mom gently kissed her on the forehead and secured her in her seatbelt to make sure she was safe.

She loved her kids and promised that after this was over, she would never allow them to be separated again until they were grown up and ready to be on their own. Bro Bro got into his seat, mom closed the door, and I began to drive. I listened to the sound of them crying and it sounded like waterfalls in my back seat. It lasted several minutes before Sally stopped crying. Unfortunately, by the time she stopped crying, there was just a short drive left before we dropped her brother off.

When I pulled up to the Group Home oceans of tears once again started to rush down her face as she panicked and gasped for air. She cried out to him begging him not to leave her. "Bro, Bro, please don't leave me. Stay with me Bro, Bro." It was so hard for her brother to leave her like that, he kept reassuring her that they would see each other soon. "Be good, and we will see each other next week, okay?" Speaking through her tears, she managed to get out "I will be good Bro, Bro." Please don't leave me.

Bro, Bro finally got out of the car. I only walked him to the front door and came right back to the car. She was hysterical by this time, and I tried hard to calm her down but there was no way to do so. Listening to the cries and remembering those from her mom nearly ripped my heart out.

Her cries caused me to remember the mom's pain as she asked forgiveness for having allowed them to be in this situation. Sally cried for her brother that I had already dropped off and for her mom again and again. When I finally arrived at her home, she begins to quiet down just a little, still sniffling.

I took a second and unfastened her seat belt and used my hand to wipe her tears away as I continued to hold her. I could feel the tension being released as she cried softly!

Finally, she went limp in my arms. I held her a little longer and then I slowly released her and looked into her swollen eyes and smiled. The joy in her eyes returned and I knew then that she would be ok. I took her tiny little hand and guided her to the front entrance of the facility. God had given her a peace and all I could say was, "Thank you, Heavenly Father, for allowing me to hear her voice." What a day!

Chapter 2

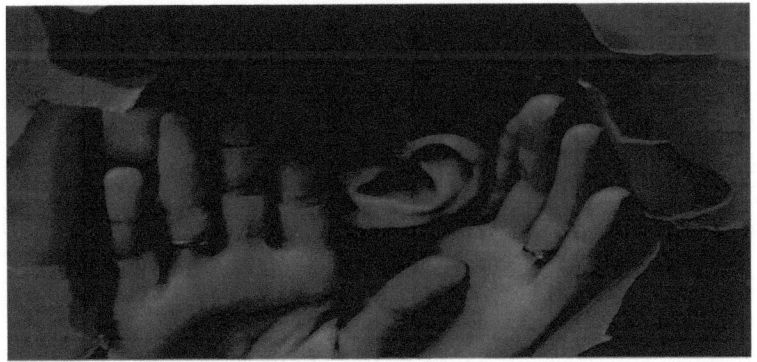

Stolen Love

My morning started off very peaceful and quiet. It was 6:00am on a Tuesday. The weather was beautiful and warm already as I touched my kitchen window. Work wise, it was like every other Tuesday when I went to the daycare to pick up two little children, a five-year old girl (Deidra) and her 18-month-old brother (Darren).

Every time I pick them up, Deidra is very excited to see me because, in her mind, she knows she's going on a visit to see her mommy and her brother, Darren. The brother is just as happy as his sister to see me. He puts both of his little arms up, staring at me with those big brown eyes, waiting for me to pick him up. I, of course, complied with his demands, and carried him to the car.

Cindy follows along as she excitedly tells me all about her day. She stands next to me as I put her brother in his car seat and secure him in his seat belt. Then, I reach for her little hand and together we walk to her side of the car. She continues telling me about daycare, her many friends, and the different activities that they have there.

I gently picked her up, put her in her car seat, and we took off to see her mom. While my favorite jazz is playing softly, Cindy continues to talk randomly.

I interrupted Cindy with the announcement of picking up her 12-year-old brother, Thomas. "Cindy, we are almost at Thomas's place." Cindy perks up even more.

Thomas is an interesting little boy who appears to carry the weight of the world on his shoulders. I find this to be very sad, because children should not have to contend with the weight of the world, adults have that responsibility. It seems that his priority is to protect his siblings and it has been like this for some time. He takes the role of protector seriously, so he doesn't smile, but he has eyes that cry without tears. When he speaks, he does so with authority as he addresses his sister.

When I ask about his day, it's often difficult for him to communicate on a casual basis. When he does, he only speaks to his sister in their native tongue. You see, they are Ethiopian, and their religion is Muslim. They live in a faraway strange land. They were taken by their parents on a visit to our land. They are living in a home that's totally unfamiliar to their culture and beliefs. It appears that he is the only one that has not adjusted to the change, and he continues to hold onto to the promises that his parents gave him the last time he saw them.

They promised that they would come for them and take them home to Ethiopian. It had been six months, but Thomas is holding onto his promises for dear life. I am hopeful that this will change someday soon.

I continued to take them to their visit with their parents. We drive to the mom's home where she is preparing a home-cooked meal, Ethiopian style. She prepared a place on the floor for them to eat as if they were in their country. Culturally, they eat with their hands while seated on the floor. Mom and the oldest boy speak to each other in Somali. While she fingers feeds the baby boy his food, the sister asks for silverware because that is now her comfort zone while enjoying her mother's presence.

Mom suddenly begins to speak in English to her son, telling him that she and his father will soon lose their parental rights. Tears slowly fall down her face as she clutches onto her baby son. The young boy looks at his mom, trying to understand what she is saying, and out of nowhere, he yells, "where is dad?" He will fix this. The sister is not affected by what's happening until she sees her brother rise from the floor, yelling, "he promised, he promised, he promised!" He then sits still in the corner, balled up in a fetal position. Mom quickly tried to change the atmosphere but was very unsuccessful. The damage was done, and severe sadness and disappointment hovered strongly in the air.

By now the session was scheduled to end and everybody's emotions were all over the place. Uncertainty was hanging in the balance, empty promises were ringing in the air, and at this point, Thomas could see no future.

Mom tried to comfort him in their native language, but the boy just stared at her dejectedly. I started to gather the kids and prepare them ready to leave for the DCS Office (Department of Children's Services).

As we walked out to leave, we noticed that the parent's vehicle was blocking my car and right then the father jumped out of it as we walked along. The father quickly walks over to his son and begins to talk to him in their language while mom gives out affection to all of them! She talks to her daughter tenderly as she puts the little ones into their car seats. The father continues to talk to Thomas in the Samali language... and then suddenly, the parents walked back to the car seats, took the two smaller kids out of them, and commanded Thomas to get into their car! They kidnapped their own kids!

I was made aware that they were caught within three hours of their actions. The authorities handled dad and mom very forcefully. Sadly, the children witnessed the severe behavior.

My heart went out to them for the pain they must have been in, but surely, they must have realized that this plan was not going to work. And once again the children were taken away from their parents (in this case violently). And so, what the parents had done with the children sealed their fate. At this point, it looked like they would never see them again. Their lives were truly shattered that day and it would take a miracle to bring them out of this drama!

Chapter 3

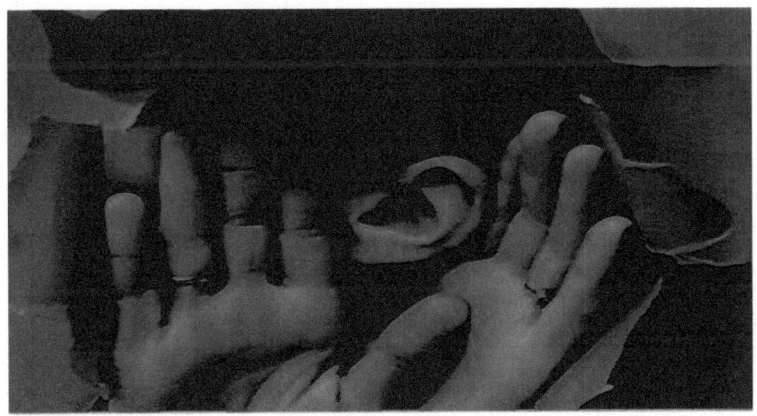

A Lost Hope

I am not sure how long my phone had been ringing, but it woke me up out of a deep sleep. Stumbling to reach for the phone, a voice screaming on the other end, "come immediately, please, hurry." After finding out who it was, I responded "it going to take me about twenty minutes to get there." The caller then said,

"You must take someone to the emergency room when you get here." My mind tried to comprehend and wake up at the same time, I remember thinking "why aren't you calling 911."

I couldn't find my keys fast enough, even though they were right in front of me. My heart raced as I started the car. I began whispering to myself "slow down and get in control of yourself!" The child I had to take to the emergency room was a 13-year-old boy. I kept hoping to myself that I would not walk into something that would totally devastate me or see a devastated child.

As I pulled up, the front door opened. I rushed and I saw Michael standing by the hallway holding his wrist that had been wrapped by staff. Fear was in his eyes. I reassured him that he would be fine as we rushed together to the car.

As I drove him to the emergency room, thoughts of our many conversations flooded my mind for some reason. Michael and I had discussed his dreams of finishing school and returning home to live with his family. He liked fishing and video games when he was not doing his homework. He also needed help in communicating his thoughts in appropriate ways that didn't end in rage. I was grateful he trusted me to care for him.

I gave him some mindful breathing exercises to help him calm down in those anxious moments.

He would tell me if he had used them from the last time, I picked him up. I would aways tell him how proud I am of him supervising himself.

I recalled a specific conversation where he became very vulnerable to me. He said he wanted to change the way that he responds to rejection. He was bullied and I personally understood the pain that he felt. "I'm tired of being alone, not being wanted," he told me. My memory lane thoughts subsided the closer we approached the hospital.

I was told to take him to this specific Emergency Room. I turn to Michael and ask, "what happened?" He answered, "I want to die." I said, "What?" Instantly, he said, "Yes!" I looked into this boy's eyes, and I saw how serious he was. I realized one day, if he stayed on this path, he would succeed. This is a 13-year-old boy who does not want to live anymore, and in his mind, death was the most feasible option.

He responded again, "I've been cutting my wrist because I want to die." He said this was not his first time trying to take his life. "I never felt loved. My parents don't love or want me because I have caused "pain" in their lives. I'm living in a place where I don't want to be. I have tried everything. No one knows what I've been through and the hurt I feel, but everybody says they understand!   I get angry, my behavior is bad, and I don't want to live. I can't go home. I am stuck with no way out but to die."

God, I heard his voice louder to end his life. I heard his pain, and I heard his powerlessness over his situation. I ached inside with no antidote but to tell him about a God who created him in His likeness and in His image. I had to tell him how much this God loved him and treasured him more than any living human being could.

Everybody around him in the group home thought that everything was fine. He appeared to be happy, engaging with everybody and doing well in school but they could not see beyond the frozen smile. They could not see the pain, agony and loneliness for his parents and to have a sense of belonging.

By this time, we had pulled up to the emergency room. I knew that once we entered, he would not come out with me. He will be on a 24-hour hold in a place where he can't hurt himself or return to the Group home. Will he be put in a severely controlled atmosphere, I wondered? They would now be watching every move he made. He would no longer have freedom like before; he would likely be drugged because he had now labeled himself as suicidal. I don't think he knew the consequences of his actions.

"Isaiah 41:10 "Fear not, for I am with you; be not dismayed, for I am your God; I will strengthen you, I will help you, I will uphold you with my righteous right hand."

To the child who thinks his life is hard and unbearable, please hold on because your life is precious and purposeful no matter what you have been through, your heavenly Father has a plan and purpose.

I Hear Their Cries

Chapter 4

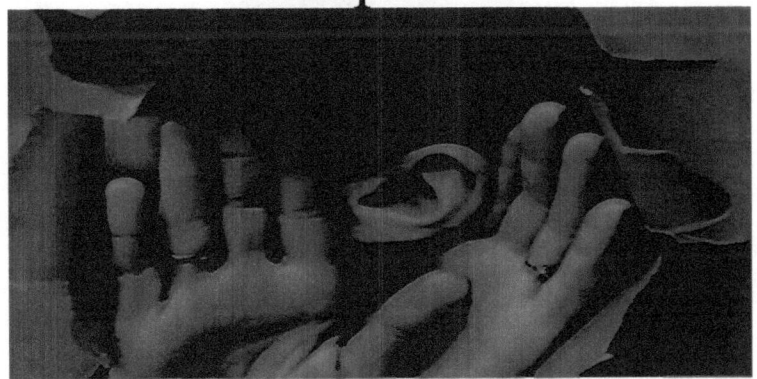

Dejavue

Reviewing my intake sheet, I saw a name on the referral that jumped out at me. It sounded so very familiar, but I eventually brushed it off because I could not place a face with the name.

Later that morning, when I picked up the 14yr old, I immediately remembered who he was. My heart was touched with joy. He remembered me too and had this big smile on his face.   He was the boy that was always angry. When he spoke, you could feel the hurt and the tears behind his words.   He was mad at his mom for allowing them to be in foster care and being taken away from his home and everything he knew! His sister was only one at the time.

It's amazing how life comes full circle at times. Just when you think you will never see a person again, you just never know the journey and God's plan. We traveled to pick up his sister and off we went making small talk and catching up.

From his location, we went to pick up his sister and boy was I surprised at her development also. The last time I saw her, she was only 1 year old. She had changed tremendously over the last four years.
Life has a way of causing us to reflect on not only our decisions, but the decisions

others make. Their mom was in so much pain 4 years ago all she could see is that she was not fit to have children or even take care of them. She gave them up not fully understanding the emotional and psychological impact it would have on them. Her broken marriage based on deception and lies got the best of her. The domestic violence left her with few choices but to try and get free and run.

At the time, she did the best that she could with what she had, which was not much after she left fleeing for her safety and the safety of her children.

Even though her children were in the system, she was still trying to correct the unfixable. She kept trying, and the darkness continued to consume her. At some point, she stopped fighting and checked out on life. Her children have been in the DCS system for four years already. After two suicide attempts to take her own life, she finally gave up and said, 'Fine, I will live' and see what comes of my life."

The little girl let's call her Debra, is now four years old and she can walk, but she communicates with sign language. She was beaten along with her mother in the womb in that domestic violent marriage.

She is barely starting to formulate words, but no complete sentences. The 14-year-old boy, however, is thriving. It's very obvious he has done some work, and God allowed a positive person to impact him for good.

After the supervised visit, I was in tears with the beautiful transformation I could see in all three. Something great has happened, and boy, it was wonderful to see.

It took the mother four years to get her life in order, working on her strength and power, determined to be able to fight for the kids. She has finally come around to doing what it takes to get them out of the system. She is now able to be a presence of love and stability for the children. I am hoping that the words "too little, too late" will not ring in the air.

---

2 Corinthians 4:8: "We are pressed on every side by troubles, but we are not crushed. We are perplexed but not driven to despair."

Psalm 40:2: "He lifted me out of the pit of despair, out of the mud and the mire. He set my feet on solid ground and steadied me as I walked along."

To all mothers whose children are part of the system: It's never too late to turn your life around. God will strengthen you and you and make a way out of no way. He is a way maker, trust Him.

Chapter 5

A Reflection of Belonging

I want to invite you to just imagine yourself waking up on an average day as a twelve-year-old boy, assuming that the world would not be any different today than yesterday.

The sun is shining bright, you are out playing with your friends by noon time on a Saturday. Your life is exciting and promising, and within a blink of an eye, everything has changed right in front of you without any rhyme or reason!

Devastation comes crashing down on your head. The person you're looking for, your protector, your safe person, the one you trust, is nowhere to be found. You have no idea what's going on, you begin to feel numb while you look at the chaos building around you, and no one is telling you what's going on. You go into protection mode, no eye contact, head down, no words, and if words were necessary, you simply nod. When the answer is yes, you shake your head to answer "no."

Strangers are now surrounding you to take you to a "safe place" away from all that you've ever called home as long as you can remember to a totally unfamiliar place!

Your new home now is a Group Home with boys you don't even know or care to know.

You are informed that you are about to have a visitor and you are hoping it is your parents who you long to see. Instead, it's another stranger. You just look but you never open your mouth to speak to them.

I picked up this timid-looking 12-year-old boy named James who did not speak much. When I introduced myself, he did not respond right off. He was quiet until he chose the moment to respond. When he did speak up, you could barely hear him. It appeared that he was tired. When I looked into his eyes, I saw a deep emptiness that rattled me. I never saw the absence of life in a child before. We drove in silence for a long time.

We finally arrived at the location of visitation. Once we were out of the car, a tall thin man walked towards us. I looked at James, and he remained silent almost as if he was a stranger to James.

After introducing myself to him, I learn that the man was his father, but he didn't seem happy to see us there. It appeared that he was angry that he had to have a visit with James. They both avoided eye contact and I could hear and see that James did not know this man at all.

This was the first day he discovered this man was his biological father. What a shock to both of us. He also found out that his mother was no longer in the picture.

James did not speak or look up or give any emotion to what he had been told. He answered "yes" and "no" when questioned or perhaps just nodded.

The father had attempted to talk with him but grew impatient and gave up. James was allowed to go out to the playground to play.

The Father simply sat on the bench and watched his son play with the other kids until the visit ended. He informed me this was his first time ever seeing James. "The evidence does not lie," he angrily stated.

According to this father, he was at a very uncomfortable fork in the road. He muttered that he already had a family and asked me, "What am I going to do with him and what am I supposed to tell my wife and children?"

Looking around, he noticed that James had come near and heard everything that he said.

On the way back to the Group home, James cried softly. I saw him in my mirror wiping the tears from his face. I asked about his visit with his father and how he felt about him. He stated, "I never saw him in my life before. It was my first time. He doesn't seem to want to be bothered with me." I probed, "Why you say that, James?" James was quiet for a minute and then said, "I don't belong to know one. No one wants me and my home now is a Group home with strangers. That is my life." James continued as if to comfort me, "I will be alright, though" as he turned to look out the car window into the darkness. I went home deeply saddened and heavy.

Psalm 130.

"Out of the depths, I cry to you, O Lord; O Lord, hear my voice. Let your ears be attentive to my cry for mercy .... I wait for the Lord, my soul waits, and in his word, I put my hope."

Proverbs 23:18 "Surely there is a future, and your hope will not be cut off."

For the twelve-year-old boy: Your life is not over. You were put on this earth to do great things.

Stephanie Liggins

I Hear Their Cries

Chapter 6

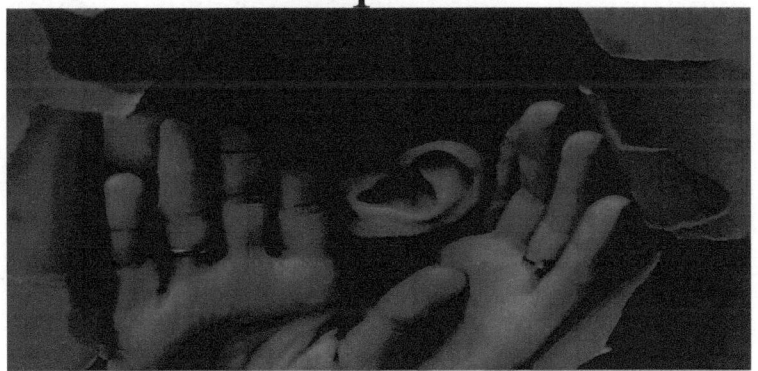

A Broken Village

I want to introduce you to a bright young girl by the name of Bridgette. She is 14 years of age going on 25. She is 14years old but seems wise beyond her years.

Bridgette told me her story when I first met her about how she ended up with her grandparents. I want to share her story with you.

On a Saturday afternoon Bridgette was experiencing her favorite pass time which was being with all her family. This included her mom, grandparents and extended family and community.

Everyone had gathered in the back yard to maximize the space for everyone to fit. Everyone gathered in the backyard to make the most of the available space. Bridget watched her mom and friends set up and prepare for the family gathering, helping here and there.

Upon everyone's arrival, the music started, the laughter filled the air and before long, card tables and dominos were ringing in the air with competitive trash talking. It was all harmless but that's just what they did according to Bridgette.

All the kids played together because they understood, staying out of grown folk's conversations.

Bridgette's grandparents did not disappoint by bringing the traditional turkey, barbecue, greens, and yams that you could smell blocks away. They knew how to cook that southern Louisiana food.

The coolers were filled with assorted drinks, sodas for the young people and beers and wine coolers for the adults.

You could hear all the oldies but goodies including Marvin Gaye, Diana Ross, Luther Vandross, Aretha Franklin and of course baby boy Stevie Wonder, Bridgette's favorite artist.

Bridgette always made fun of the grown people dancing. She loved to dance with her mother and aunties as they exchanged partners looping her in to all the 2-step cha cha's. Bridgette was very close to her mother, and it was nothing she could not talk to her about. This gave Bridgette comfort and confidence.

Suddenly, amid the festivities and fun, a different kind of sound pierced the atmosphere. Voices were raised in aggressive tones. At first Bridgette ignored continuing to play with her sister and brother. Then she heard her mother's voice in a different tone using strong language. Her voice was louder than the music and everyone could hear her. Bridgette described how she was talking to her father (Bridgette's grandfather). She could see her mom and grandfather across the yard. Then from the corner of her eyes her mother appeared to be fighting with her very own father and that's when everyone began to run toward them to break it up.

Bridgette's mother ran away and left the house immediately after the physical altercation. The next thing Bridgette saw was policemen flood the back yard. At first no one knew who called the police, until the neighbors began to show up looking at the disturbance. The officers approached Bridgette's grandfather and commenced to talk with him about the fight.

Little by little everyone began to leave the family gathering. The last song was playing by Glady's Night "Neither one of us wants to be the first to say goodbye." Bridgette will never forget that moment.

Sitting on the porch now quiet, afraid, and worried, Bridgette and her siblings watched everyone leave, one by one. Just moments ago, laughter, fun and dancing filled the backyard. Their youthful bliss was snatched in a moment of distress. As each family member left, they motioned their good-byes to Bridgette and her siblings.

Next, Bridgette's grandmother motions for the kids to go into the house.

Bridgete could still hear the whispers saying, "she's gone officer, she just left, and we do not know where she went."

A couple of hours later, the house phone rang, and it was the police station informing Bridgette's grandparents that they had found their daughter and she was in custody.   Bridgette's grandmother begins to cry, and her grandfather holds her in his arms.

With sadness in his voice, Grandfather said to her grandmother, "you know we will have to take the kids with us tonight and figure everything out." Grandmother said, "at our age? I never thought we would be raising children in our 70s."

Bridgette questioned, "what does all of this mean?" Is mom gone for good? Will she ever come back? What's really going to happen to us?

Bridgette became very angry and resentful at this sudden change in her family's life. Admittedly, she shared her life was perfect, but at least she knew what to expect.

She was fully aware that her mom was not the best, but she was the only mom she had. There were times when she had to compete for her mother's affection and time. There were always extra people around her. If it was not the people, then it was her mom's substance abuse that put a wedge of neglect in their home.

Nonetheless, Bridgette found herself taking care of not only her siblings, but also her mom when she was unable to care for herself due to substance. Bridgette understood what it meant to be parentified at a young age.

Just when Bridgette thought things had slowed down and her mom was home more often, then a new man enters her mom's life consuming all her time and resources. Bridgette witnessed the viscous cycle of feelings of abandonment and neglect.

So now, Bridgette is feeling the burden of her grandparents' actions toward them, which makes her feel powerless to fix or do anything about it. She sees two representations of her grandparents which is very confusing to her. Some days she feels they are welcomed and most days she feels their anger and resentment that they now must raise their daughter's kids. Anger stirs in Bridgette more and more to the point of her behavior changing toward her grandparents who she loved.

So, when I asked Bridgette, how did they end up in DCS (Of course, I already knew), she was very honest with me. "I didn't want to do anything they asked me to do because I felt like they didn't want us there anyway. I was rebellious and disrespected them by my language and cursing. Then I would lie and manipulate so that I could get my way even if I had to play them against each other. One day, I even took some money out of my grandmother's purse, and I believe that was the straw that broke the camel's back.

The next thing I knew, strange people were at the door to pick us up. My parents tried to make it sound nice as if I really didn't do anything, they blamed it all on their age in front of us, but I know they told those people the truth of how I was acting.

And so that day everything changed. I thought all 3 of us would still be together, tears flowing down her face."

I gently touched her hands, "I'm very sorry to hear that, Bridgette. You and your siblings have had a very hard journey. And you are correct, you went to a Group home due to the information they received about your behavior. And your brother went to his father's mom's home.

So now your mother is out of jail, and you are mad at the fact that her first stop was not to come and get you guys back but instead, try to hook back up with your brother's father.

Bridgette responded angrily, "yes, I am mad because she always chooses everyone else over us! That's what she always does! "That must hurt. I understand your anger. If I were you, I would probably feel the same emotions that you are going through.

Bridgette wiped her face and said, "why do I get so angry, this is nothing new." Because you never thought she would choose him over your sister and yourself." "No, I guess I didn't think that could happen at this point. I thought she would be so happy to get out and get her family back. I was wrong."

I knew Bridgette had a lot to get off her chest and I just sat there to listen and to normalize and to support her.

Did you know that it took my mom 6 months to make provisions to visit the two us?" Every night all I wanted was for my mom and me and my siblings to be back together as a family again!!

Then to throw gas on fire, when she was scheduled to visit with us, one cancellation after another, one excuse after another. I stopped believing she would ever come."

I felt this was an appropriate time to join the conversation to validate Bridgette's feelings. "I will never forget one time; I got a call that your mom would not be visiting you two today. I was standing in front of you and your sister, and her eyes were glimmering and filled with joy. Your sister had a gift for your mom, and she couldn't wait to give it to her.

It hurt my heart to have to tell those beautiful girls who had been waiting almost a year that she would not be here today.

I knew they would ask me why and as I saw how happy and excited; they were to see their mom and to go to their visit I couldn't tell them the truth... that their mom did not want to have a visit today.

I just could not do it and so I told them that their mom was sick and could not come. Still, the oldest girl knew that was not the truth. She turned and said, "I bet my brother sees mom, but when it's our turn, she comes up with an excuse."

I could see the anger building up, and the tears that would not fall from her eyes as she headed back into the Group home holding her sister's hand. The happiness left their hearts and was replaced with darkness and disappointment.

The girls' visit with their mom finally came and they had an additional surprise to see their baby brother with her.

They enjoyed their visit and loved being with their mom and one another. They made sure they had lots of fun.

←——————————————————————→

Romans 12:21 "Do not be overcome by evil but overcome evil with good."

Zephaniah 3:17 "The Lord your God in your midst, the Mighty One, will save; He will rejoice over you with gladness, He will quiet you with His love, He will rejoice over you with **singing**."

To the unseen children who were parentified before your time, keep your head up. Resist the destructive words and actions of others. Choose to hope today.

Chapter 7

A Mother's Search for Hope

Here is a mother whose name is Teresa. She finds herself in a difficult situation because she tried something that sealed her fate forever. Crack Cocaine is not a casual social drug. It's an all or nothing drug. Teresa didn't know the first hit would land her in an early gradual grave robbing her from her dignity, respect, family and purpose.

Her 6year-old and 13year-old child are suddenly faced with a new mother who comes home and can no longer pay attention to them as she used to.

In fact, after their daughters would come home from school, they would find their mother locked in a room or go most of the night with people that they've never seen. Mother's new friends look dangerous and desperate. The activities that they engage in are always secretive. Now the girls are wondering to themselves, "what are all the people doing in the back in their mother's room?" Next, she stops coming home all together.

One day the teenage girl comes home from school to find her mother sitting on the porch with her younger sister with a large bag. She doesn't understand what's going on. The first words that she hears from her mother is, "we have to leave baby, we can't stay here." Her daughter drops her head in confusion and fear asking a million questions from her mother only to be shut down and yelled at.

Then Teresa begins to walk off the property and her daughters follow behind her. They soon notice that she is walking endlessly with no destination in mind. The girls are now afraid to ask their mom, "where are we going since the last yelling episode."

Imagine, my dear readers what these young girls are going through:

The sun is setting, it's getting dark, and their mother tells them that, "I have to find you guys a place to sleep for the night." She finally finds a spot that appears to be secure enough for the night… it is an empty room with an empty cement floor. She pulls out the blankets that are in the duffle bag and instructs her daughters to lay down on the floor.

It's sad, it's uncomfortable, and it's not home. The 13-year-old realizes dinner is not coming.

At the same time, I try to keep my girl's spirits up while I gather the covers. I think about how I will feed them. The questions ring in my ear as to how I will feed them with no money. I decided that it couldn't get any worse. I go to a supermarket and begin to ask for change in the parking lot. I did not know that someone had called the police, and they came, detained you and took your kids. You were incarcerated, and now you are out and don't know where the girls are.

It is Sunday. You begin to shut down! Your lifeline is no longer there. You can't breathe or eat. You find yourself surrounded by people you should not be with. You survived that day, and now you are desperately trying to find your daughters… and now a week has gone by, and by chance, you received information that they are in the system DCS.

You must figure out how to get them out. It is not easy and now a week has turned into three before you finally get the information from the DCS. A case manager has been assigned to you, and you must go through that person to get your information. You have no phone; the department is closed now, and it will be another day before you can call. You are going crazy not knowing where your girls are, and you are still homeless.

It's Friday morning, you are standing in front of the entrance of the DCS building, waiting for it to open for business. The Door opens you wait to see the Case Manger assigned to your case. It's been all morning, and no one has called you. You are pacing the floor and trying not to show anger while you continue to wait. The Case Manager's finally called you as you sit in the office, listening to someone who does not know you, tell you that you will not see your (2) girls because they do not want to see you. This person says that they are happy living with strangers. Now the case worker tells you that your thirteen-month-old is not living in the same house as her sister. You do not know where your girls are, but you know that they are not together! You continue to listen to this woman that has all this power over your life… and your children's lives—giving you information as to why you will not get them back at this point.

A treatment plan was written up, advising you of the things you have to do in order to get them back. You have no idea what it all means; all you know is that this person said that you must complete this list before you see the Judge in two mouths. We want to let you know that a visitation has been set up weekly with your fourteen-month-old daughter. You leave the office in a daze, confused because it really does not make sense as to why you do not have your kids. It has been a month since you have seen your girls, heard their voices and laughter, embraced and told them how much you love them. And now, you are homeless, have a list of items you must complete before you can get them back. At this moment, with all this pain, you just can't take it anymore. So, you check out and numb your pain. You don't realize how long you were out of it, but you know you haven't done all that was required! And now it's time to see the judge. You stand in front of him… the one who is reading to you all the charges in your file.

The file went back through five years of your life, and everything came full circle. The cost of your action is that now you are homeless, and your girls are in the system. You went into denial once you heard what was against you, but the evidence was right there before you. The Judge gave you instructions, set up visitations that were effective immediately with your fourteen-month-old daughter and scheduled a court appointment three months from now.

Now you are angry that you have people in your life telling you how to live it, and they took your girls away from you because of what they think they know about you. The next time you see your baby girl, she is fifteen months old; she is not speaking, just making sounds. Tears flowed like an ocean from your eyes as you held her closely to your chest. You were afraid to breathe because this might have been a dream. You kept her close... but she wanted to play with you as you sat on the floor. You held her near wanting to watch her every move.

Future visits were the same with non-stop tears running down your face and only you knew why. Sometimes the tears were unseen, but people could hear it in your voice.

You began to work on your treatment plan. It's two months away from court day. You are not homeless anymore. You were searching for a job. You became comfortable seeing your baby girl every week, which gave you hope to try harder. Your Case Manager reached out to you to give you your progress report regarding what you should have completed, but for the most part, it was not a good report and court was in a week. The case manager read your parental rights as mentioned in the report. You think that what she is saying cannot be right because as you understand it, you have accomplished everything that the judge told you to do.

Finally, court day is here, and you are standing in front of the Judge. Your mouth hangs open as he states that he is revoking your parental rights. In your head you scream that you did too little too late. His voice echoes in your ear that you are no longer the mother of your girls, and you will never see them again. Your whole demeanor was shaken at this outcome. You sat there with tears forming in your eyes while processing what the Judge has just said before walking out of the courtroom.

←――――――――――――――――――――――→

Jeremiah 30:17 "But I will restore you to health and heal your wounds,' declares the Lord."

Proverbs 23:18 "Surely there is a future, and your hope will not be cut off."

To the Parents that find themselves overwhelmed by their current situation… You have the power to choose to change your ways… for yourself and your children… make that change knowing that your children today will soon be adults and one day will come looking for you. I urge you to make the change, correct your lifestyle! Be ready to show them that the loss of your special children was what you needed to get to where you are today! You can show them that the pain of their loss was almost more than what you could take… and so you cleaned up your life and if they will allow it, you can be a wonderful family.

Do you hear their cries?   Draw closer, see them, they are everywhere: In our communities, our churches, our schools and in our very own families. I invite you to open your compassionate heart and ears to hear their cries and empower and encourage them of their God-given worth. Join the fight for healthy families and reunification.

About the Author

Stephanie Liggins is a compassionate caring clinician. Her new book reveals the essence of her heart for hurting families, especially vulnerable children. She entered into this helping career to make a difference in the reunification of families. Stephanie counts it a privilege and honor to journey with families striving to mend the broken places and spaces of their lives.

Professionally as a Case Aide, she has impacted empowered and encouraged children with her natural flowing compassionate heart. With the pen of a ready writer, she uplifts downtrodden heads with words of possibilities, resilience, and hope. Stephanie believes the gift of healing comes from the capacity to have empathy for others that unlocks the chained soul.

She serves on the Executive Board of Vessouls of Transformation Sisters of Change a woman's Black owned Organization who advocates for the eradication of Human Trafficking while also advocating for Diversity, Equity and Inclusion rights in historically marginalized communities.

Ms. Liggins is passionate about her personal relationship with Jesus Christ and serves at the Seventh-Day-Adventist Church.

www.ingramcontent.com/pod-product-compliance
Lightning Source LLC
Chambersburg PA
CBHW020335130626
46549CB00003B/1181